# Haiku Happy You.

# Prescribed Positivity.

# Poems to Inspire.

By *Michael Alexander*
Cover art by *Katrina Carroll-Haskins*

"*Haiku Happy You.*

*Prescribed Positivity.*

*Poems to Inspire.*" © 2019 by **Michael Alexander.**

Cover art © 2019 by **Katrina Carroll-Haskins.**

Proofreaders: **Beth DeJong & Patricia Grabowski**

ISBN: 9781707892594

Library of Congress Control Number: 2020900396

All rights reserved. No part of this book may be reproduced or transmitted in any form or by any means without written permission from the author.

HaikuHappyYou@hotmail.com

www.Facebook.com/HaikuHappyYou

*Kindle Direct Publishing*

*Amazon.com Services LLC*

*410 Terry Ave N, Seattle, WA 98109*

The traditional haiku captures our observations of natural settings and everyday occurrences, with frogs jumping or rain falling being two cliché examples. The form has the virtues of simplicity, brevity and memorability. They can usually be enjoyed by themselves and in any order, as if we're eating a box of chocolates. Notably, the focus is usually on *external* events in the world *around* us.

But in Mike Alexander's haiku, no doubt shaped by his years of practice in clinical psychology, we see a special shift in focus to *internal* events -- the automatic thoughts and emotional reactions evoked by our perceptions of threats or opportunities and our recollections of traumas or triumphs. In short, these haiku are primarily about the world *within* us and how we process it. They capture the juxtaposition between our unexamined inner life and our reflective mind.

This structural development can represent our personal evolution as we read them, and perhaps it can even enable further growth if we get into the habit of composing our own in this style. In addition to the usual qualities of traditional haiku, the psychological variations found in this book possess a uniquely therapeutic quality: the potential for important insight, maybe even aphoristic wisdom.

-Vincent J. Alia, November 2019

Now I present to you,

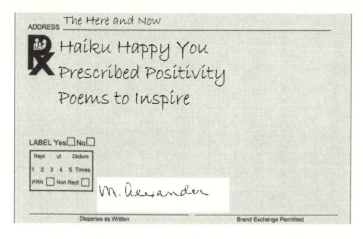

I have worked in the social services field for a number of years. In the close to 15 years, I've worked with children suffering from depression, who've experienced trauma, had significant impulse and anger control problems, displayed a lack of self-identity and worth, didn't feel as though they "belonged", and, because of their past, had difficulty trusting people. I'd like to think that through some of the work I've done with them, I played some minor role in the successful, happy, productive adults that many of them have become. I feel as though that is my calling. I want to help people realize their self-worth and importance, even when others are doing their best to do just the opposite. I want to help others find their own happiness, and to recognize that this is an ongoing journey, not a destination to reach.

I too have been where many of the children were/are. Through my own therapeutic process, and the assistance of some great self-help books, I found personal strength and a new insight. I was inspired, motivated, and made aware of my own self-worth. And through philosophical readings and conversations, I've gained a different outlook on life, and how I react to various situations and events that may come my way, and are beyond my control. It's not always easy, but it's doable. Here I'd like to continue my quest in trying to help others gain a new perspective.

One day, as I sat in the corner of a dimly lit pub reading a book of haiku, most of which were random nonsense, the idea hit me. Why not write a book of haiku that provided people with some take away sense of usefulness and satisfaction? A book of haiku with meaning and purpose that some might read and think to themselves, "Wow. This really 'speaks' to me". A collection of haiku that might brighten one's day, change a particular course, or even alter a certain mindset in which you may find yourself.

Let us not get too bogged down on an exact definition of "haiku". Here's what I mean, and what most of us learned in grade school. It's a short 3 line poem in a syllabic 5:7:5 pattern. Some of the following poems may involve nature (as you might read as being one of the characteristics of a traditional haiku); but many of them do not fit this trait. What I wish for all who read the contents within to understand is the following:

- They were written to inspire, motivate, uplift, and reframe certain ways of thinking.
- Maybe you'll feel some don't apply to you. Hopefully there are plenty that do.
- You may find similarities in many of the poems. That's ok. It's a good way to emphasize importance.
- Some haiku have underlying meanings. They are allegories for life and events we might encounter. Please take some time to think about and reflect upon them.
- Some will come off as my advice to you, the reader. Take it or leave it.

- Some are subjective. You may derive one meaning, personal to you, while someone else embraces a different meaning, personal to them.
- And finally- If you've enjoyed and/or benefitted from these haiku in any way, please share them and the book with loved ones- friends and family.

*This book is meant to provide some hope, spread positivity, inspire, and motivate the reader. It is in no way a replacement for professional assistance when/if needed.*

"What mental health needs is more sunlight, more candor, more unashamed conversation about illnesses that affect not only individuals, but their families as well." Glenn Close

## **HAPPINESS**

For some it is rain.

Others enjoy the riches.

I seek the mundane.

## **FAMILY**

They are there for me.

Through the good times and the bad.

I love each of you.

## **FOOD**

Refrigerator.

Filled with all kinds of good food.

I won't go hungry.

## **HOME**

The dark sky rumbles.

The winds howl ferociously.

Inside I am safe.

## NATURE

Beauty of nature.

Sunlight breaking through the trees.

Here I am at peace.

## ANGER

Heart has been broken.

My inner peace will remain.

I will not falter.

## SIMPLICITY

Don't need many things.

A simple life is my goal.

Greed is a monster.

## CHOICES

Choose to be happy,

when life takes an awkward turn.

Don't let go of joy.

## SOCIAL TIME

Being among friends.

Drinking, laughing, having fun.

Great times had by all.

## SURROUNDINGS

The birds are chirping.

Oh, what wonderful music.

Summer time is here.

## LIVE YOUR LIFE

Death smiles at us all.

Enjoy life to the fullest.

Que sera sera.

## COMFORT ZONE

I asked some questions.

Despite my anxiety.

Work meeting goal met.

## HUMANITY

Whether rich or poor,

Black, white, boy, girl, or famous;

We are all human.

## DAD

This past Father's Day,

I remembered my father.

Both father and dad.

## GO!

Get up. Get moving!

Stillness is the enemy.

Work mind and body.

## HEY, HI.

Casual hellos.

Enough to start a convo.

Most people don't bite.

## MEANING.

Meaningful work goals-

At times you are productive-

Here's where you belong.

## A LIFE OF ORGANIZED TIME

Organize your thoughts.

Eliminate the excess.

De-clutter your life.

## DON'T WORRY

"What- ifs" are toxic.

Intrusive thoughts invade minds.

Learn to let these go.

## KEEP IT REAL

Reach for the bright stars.

Before that, reach for the moon.

First, set Earthly goals.

## OPTIMISM PRIME

I've suffered defeats.

I've been beaten and battered.

I've weathered the storms.

## A PRESENT FOR YOU

Tomorrow you're not-

Yesterday is but a dream.

What to do right now?

## PERSONALITY PRESCRIPTION

Treat others kindly.

Find humor in trying times.

Spread cheer and wisdom.

## HELLO WORLD

A 'hi' to strangers,

can lead to lasting friendships.

Don't dismiss this chance.

## BE YOURSELF

Be like your sister.

Pressure to be like others.

Just be who you are.

## MAKE THE CUT

Negativity.

Eliminate this feeling.

Seek the positive.

## WATER TO GROW

Close relationships:

Are important to maintain.

Nourish to help grow.

## WHAT'S IT WORTH?

Value happiness.

It is our ultimate goal.

Cherish what's valued.

## IDLE LIVES

Invest energy,

into doing things you like.

Become more active.


## TOP OF THE MORNING

Walking in the park.

A stranger passes by me.

We greet each other.


## BLUEPRINTS

Planning out your day.

So that things may go smoothly.

This may cause less stress.


## THREE LITTLE BIRDS

A song comes to mind.

Don't worry about a thing.

My message to you.

## EXPECTATIONS VS. REALITY

I expect respect.

But sometimes I don't get it.

It is what it is.

## ON THE OTHER HAND…

The storm killed some trees.

Basements and roads were flooded.

But no one was hurt.

## LEARN TO LET GO

I once had someone-

Who I loved and respected.

But that was the past.

## LOOK INWARD

What traits to look for,

when in search of another?

Build these in yourself.

## GOING OUT

Self-isolation.

Can be quite a lonely life.

Get out in the world.


## IT'S ALL WE CAN DO

Just to be yourself.

It's the thing we can all do.

Don't think otherwise.


## THE PLAGUE

Negative feelings.

Plague our minds like a cancer.

Eliminate them.


## HOMEMADE WITH LOVE

A warm home cooked meal.

Where family sits to eat.

This brings me true joy.

## THE SECRET

A secret is this:

Truly value happiness.

Attainment follows.


## BE A HAPPINESS INVESTOR

Put more into life.

You will get more out of it.

Allow time for fun.


## IT'S ONLY AN EMOTION

What is happiness?

It's not the material,

but an emotion.


## FAREWELL SOFA

On this gorgeous day,

I decided to go play.

My couch misses me.

## TECHNOLOGY FREE

Sitting for a meal.

Does not include cell phone use.

Talk with each other.

## MY PRESCRIPTION FOR YOU

By writing poems,

I hope to inspire you all.

Your turn to inspire.

## FROM ME TO YOU

Here's one more haiku.

It's all about happiness

My poem for you.

## IT'S UP TO YOU

They said you wouldn't.

Become what you want to be.

Who are they to say?

## TRUE FRIENDS

Friends can come and go.

True friends are with you always.

So choose them wisely.


## VALUE

Know what you are worth,

not what others determine.

It is not their call.


## KEEP IT REAL

I broke someone's heart.

And had my heart broken too.

But it still pumps blood.


## IN THE NOW

Goodbye Yesterday.

You're a time I can't get back.

I live in the now.

## POSITIVE SPIN

Bills can be a pain.

A burden we must endure.

At least we have them.


## FOR YOU

Time spent with nephew.

At first he whined and complained.

His smile was worth it.


## WINDS OF CHANGE

Winds of change will blow.

Sometimes hard, sometimes often.

Best prepare your base.


## STAY AFLOAT

Willful ignorance.

In a vast sea of knowledge.

It's a choice to drown.

## **PERSIST**

I think of others.

Often not thought of by them.

My thoughts will persist.

## **SHINE ON**

Stars' lights shine brightly.

I too aim to shine brightly-

Long after I'm gone.

## **INNER PEACE**

Find your inner peace.

Then help others find their own.

This gives us purpose.

## **CONTAGION**

Happy and upbeat.

Let these people surround you.

It is contagious.

## THE STRUGGLE'S REAL

When you are struggling.

Do not suffer in silence.

Learn to talk it out.


## HAPPY TEARS

Find reasons to laugh.

Do as often as you can.

Laugh until tears flow.


## SWIM FARTHER

Broaden horizons.

Move beyond the safe shoreline.

Absorb all you can.


## AT ONE

Beauty of nature.

Awe and a sense of oneness.

We are part of it.

## UNTO OTHERS

Doing for others.

When there's opportunity.

Let this be your goal.

## WASTED

Don't waste energy-

On those who treat you poorly.

Keep your inner peace.

## US VS. THEM

Us and them thinking.

Fan flames of intolerance.

Learn from history.

## CHISEL

Words on paper fade.

Those on stone one day erode.

Ingrain words on minds.

## **CONSTELLATIONS**

Systems of support.

Good for your mind and body.

Rely on self too.

## **BON APPETITE**

Cooking for loved ones.

Sustains me in many ways.

Now, bon appétit.

## **TRY THIS**

Just apologize-

When you should, give when you can,

Smile and give daily.

## **CHOOSE HAPPINESS**

Your own happiness.

Begins from within yourself.

It's a choice you make.

## **LOOK BEFORE YOU LEAP**

Conclusion jumping.

Use caution when doing so.

Know where you're landing.

## **RUNGS**

High expectations.

Climbing far up this ladder,

Can lead to great falls.

## **STRENGTH**

Be humble and true.

Acknowledge your weaknesses.

This is your true strength.

## **TURN BACK TIME**

Time with family.

Is time that should be cherished.

We can't get it back.

## FOSTER

Drop hate and anger.

They eat away at our core.

Don't foster these two.


## BEST FRIEND

What they think of you-

Should not be the guide for thoughts.

Be your own best friend.


## IMPULSE

Impulsive actions-

Before taking time to think-

Can lead to conflict.


## DOWN THE DRAIN

Choose people wisely.

Embrace positivity.

Others are a drain

## SEEKER

Read much and often.

Seek for your inspiration.

Then find your own words.

## LIGHT IT UP

Be one who inspires.

Words and actions like lightning.

You shall cause thunder.

## KNOW IT ALL

You should know enough—

You will never know it all.

But don't stop learning.

## LISTEN HERE

Be charitable.

Apologize when you should.

Smile and love often.

## PLANTED

High expectations.

Can lead to a fall from high.

Stay firmly planted.

## LOOK WITHIN

Your own happiness.

Begins from within yourself.

It's a choice we make.

## LIMITED

Be humble and true.

Know your own limitations.

This is your power.

## SACRED

Hanging with loved ones.

Talking, laughing, having fun.

Hold these times sacred.

## SACRIFICIAL

Sacrifice comfort-

If it helps comfort others.

You'll be the hero.

## SPOTTER

Do not get pulled down-

When bending to help others.

Know what you can lift.

## SAVE GRIEF

Have healthy debates.

Avoid vapid arguments.

Save yourself the grief.

## FIRM BASE

Rational thinking.

Allow it to be your base.

Such thoughts should stand strong.

## TOUR GUIDE

Haiku to inspire.

I hope each one makes you think.

Let them be your guide.

## RENDERED MOOT

Friends are family.

Those who are true are your kin.

Genetics are moot.

## DEAFENING SILENCE

Listen to silence.

Could be all you need to hear.

Silence speaks volumes.

## THE AUTHOR

You are an author.

Your own happiness, the plot.

Write a good story.

## **CONTENTS UNDER PRESSURE**

Frustration can build.

Take a step back and reflect.

This feeling shall pass.


## **FIRE STARTER**

Good books are the spark.

They can ignite a passion.

Within you the blaze.


## **PEACHES**

If some bad apples-

Spoil the bunch that's around you-

Seek out some peaches.


## **BEND**

An obstinate man-

Who is unwilling to bend-

Can easily break.

## KNOWLEDGE

Good education.

Is sometimes confused with school.

One's continual.

## STRANGLED

Strangling, grasping weeds.

Wrap around our foundation.

Won't let flowers grow.

## THOUGHT INTRUDER

Green rabbits pop in.

Green rabbits quickly pop out.

Block unwanted thoughts.

## BULLIED

Bullying is weak.

It's an outward cry for help.

It's not about you.

## SHIMMER

If darkness surrounds-

Search for that shimmer of light.

It's from those who care.

## LOGIC 101

Fallacious thinking.

Muddies waters of discourse.

Seek truth and reason.

## SCULPTURE

Sculpt your masterpiece.

Step back, think, and be patient.

Worthy goals take time.

## LIGHTHOUSES

Surrounded by doubt.

A sea of isolation.

Swim to lighthouses.

## **MAKE YOUR MARK**

Make your worldly mark-

Before the world marks you first.

Initiate change.

## **APATHY**

Ugly apathy.

Enemy of decency.

Let justice prevail.

## **NEVER-ENDING JOURNEY**

Attainment of peace.

Obtaining some happiness.

Not impossible.

## **BEG TO DIFFER**

A call of "heaven".

Might just be another's "hell".

Ok to differ.

## STURDY BRIDGES

Water under bridge.

Can cause rust and erosion.

Repair to strengthen.

## STAGNATION

Progress together.

Or we stagnate and crumble.

There's strength in numbers.

## YAWP

Your accomplishments.

Shout them aloud from rooftops.

Don't brag but inspire.

## ASTRAY

Dare to break away.

A pack can tend to guide us.

Travel your own path.

## PREVENT FOREST FIRES

Small sparks of anger-

Can lead to wildfires of rage.

This can consume us.


## LISTEN TO THE MUSIC

In life songs may end.

But the music will go on.

Listen while you can.


## CLEAR THE PATH

The pathway to truth

Can be littered with debris.

Pick up your own trash.


## SWEET REWARDS

Azalea flowers.

Insects search for sweet nectar.

A sweet goal achieved.

## HAPPINESS FLOW

Happiness will come.

Happiness will also go.

Keep a state of flow.

## REACTION TIME

Can't control all change.

When something in life changes,

Control your response.

## BEWARE IMPOSTERS

Cherish true friendships.

There for you in times of need.

Beware of the fakes.

## LET IT BE

It is what it is.

It will be what it will be.

Keep your steady course.

## POWER OF WORDS

The power of words.

Can inspire or put one down.

Choose them carefully.


## HANDLE WITH CARE

Life's fragility.

It can be cold and callous.

But kindness exists.


## BLACK HOLE

We're all streams of light.

Traveling the universe.

Beware of black holes.


## RISE ABOVE

Inspired to rise up.

To be more and to do more.

My turn to inspire.

## COMMON GROUND

Set aside dispute.

Seek common ground and pleasure.

Remember to love.

## GOOD COMPANY

It's not where you are.

It's about who you are with.

And where you're going.

## TREES OF ADVENTURE

Trees of adventure.

Take the risk to climb up high.

Swing out on a branch.

## UNEXPLORED

Stray from concrete paths.

Explore dirt trails in the woods.

But know your way back.

## BUMPY ROADS

Follow where facts lead.

This is how we get to truth.

The path may feel rough.


## IMMERSED

Sitting by a lake.

I hear ducks, bugs, and babies.

Here I am at peace.


## JUST BREATHE

Most of life is work.

Don't ignore personal joy.

Take some time to breathe.


## RIGHT NOW

When you say "someday",

Right now you should realize,

Today is that day.

## QUICK JUDGEMENTS

Absorb all knowledge.

Scientists and the homeless.

Both impart wisdom.

## CLICK

The "cool" kid table.

Not a license to be mean.

Rise above bullies.

## ONE SMALL STEP

The smallest gesture.

Can make a big difference.

Even just a smile.

## BAD TODAYS

For each bad "today",

Allow more good "tomorrows".

You can walk this path.

## INFLATION

Know what you are worth.

Not what others determine.

It is not their call.

## CHOOSE WISELY

Choose words carefully.

When speaking to those you love.

They may be the last.

## TAKE TIME

Take the time to care.

Be patient and don't give up.

You'll see the reward.

## ALIVE

Do your very best,

To not be so into life,

That you don't live it.

## PAINED

Move on, don't forget.

Be productive and engaged.

Pain felt will subside.


## MINIMIZE

Mad consumerism.

Weed choking humanity.

Try to minimize.


## BYSTANDER

"It don't affect me".

"I don't care", is flawed thinking.

Shaky moral ground.


## TEN ROUNDS

Don't ever give up!

People may disappoint you.

If you love them, fight.

## UNBEARABLE WEIGHT

Full and sole control.

This could make one unhappy.

Weight comes crashing down.


## RESOLUTIONS

New Year holiday.

Don't need one day to set goals.

Accomplish them now.


## WANTING WHAT YOU HAVE

Love what you have now.

Don't fail to appreciate.

It could all be gone.


## PAGE-TURNER

Memories remain.

Embrace them with open arms.

Learn to turn the page.

## DISTRACTION

No phones at dinner.

Technology can anchor.

Converse with others.


## YOU'RE WELCOME

Express gratitude.

When someone brightens dark paths.

Not indignation.


## HAPPY LITTLE TREES

Hold up your pallet.

See your paints, brush, and canvas.

Make a masterpiece.


## TORCHBEARER

The bright light of truth.

Shines from torches of bearers-

Scattering falsehoods.

## NO CHARGE

Worthy to pass on.

Love, empathy, compassion.

It's free to do so.


## SCARS REMAIN

Scars are reminders.

Of the battles we once fought.

Display them proudly.


## MOVE ON

Anger will subside.

Certain injuries may not.

Get mad, then move on.


## BRIDGE BUILDERS

Try building bridges.

Even with opposition.

Tear down barriers.

## BOTTLED UP

If it's not expressed,

Your problems get bottled up.

Seek a solution.

## BROVALENT BONDS

Cheers to all my friends.

Some are old and some are new.

May such bonds remain.

## LINES DRAWN

Drawn lines in the sand.

If they are being ignored,

Look for a new beach.

## BREAK THROUGH

Love and empathy.

Breaking through intolerance.

Chip away at hate.

## BIRDS OF A FEATHER

Embrace common sense.

Be decent and courteous.

Be with those like you.


## VIP PASS

You're a V.I.P

You're important to many.

Treat yourself kindly.


## BOB ROSS WOULDN'T DARE

Painting with broad strokes.

Gets paint in spots you don't want.

Know your work surface.


## WHISPERS

The faintest whisper.

Can start a rippling movement.

Start the discussion.

## SHARE KNOWLEDGE

Of moral import.

Share knowledge with each other.

Do not conceal it.

## TEND YOUR GARDEN

Allow plants to grow.

Provide water and sunlight.

Watch them sprout flowers.

## TAKE ME TO YOUR LEADER

Please hold down the fort.

I'm a five star general.

I take over forts.

## THE PERFECT YOU

Please just be yourself.

No one is as good at it.

It takes no practice.

## PART OF THE WHOLE

I am but one spoke.

In a wheel that is turning.

But I help it turn.


## DEAR DETRACTORS

Detractors of peace.

Please distance yourself from me.

Inner peace is mine.


## CIVILITY

Have civil discourse.

If you and I disagree,

We can still be cool.


## COOLER HEADS

Combat ignorance.

Don't resort to violence.

Use education.

## LEARNING CURVE

Learn to love yourself.

Learn to love loving your life.

Learn your own self-worth.


## STILL I CLIMB

Over utilized.

Under appreciated.

Still I climb upward.


## REPEAT AFTER ME

Repeat: I am strong.

I will rise above defeat.

I am determined.


## PREPAREDNESS

The future is yours.

Prep for tomorrow today.

Don't procrastinate.

## ROAD'S END

A difficult road.

May lead to something gorgeous.

Tighten your bootstraps.

## TO DO

Today's to do list.

Ignore negativity.

Let go of the past.

## I BELIEVE

To be successful:

First, believe that you can be.

This is where you start.

## DENIED ENTRY

You will get angry.

You get depressed and worried.

This won't consume you.

## LOOSEN YOUR GRIP

Strive for happiness.

Let go of sorrow's burden.

Leave the past behind.

## [DON'T] DIG IT

If you're in a hole,

First thing is to stop digging.

Be your own best friend.

## FACE IT

Problems can be solved.

Accept them, leave them, change them.

But face them head on.

## PEACE BE WITH YOU

Make peace with your past.

Don't let it disturb today.

Stay in the moment.

## CHALLENGED CLICHÉ

It's not time that heals.

It's what you do with your time.

Don't waste it away.


## WHO'S THE BOSS?

No one is in charge-

Of you becoming happy.

You are the boss here.


## NO COMPARISON

Do not compare lives.

Live the best life possible.

This is your journey.


## ALTERED VIEW

Sometimes things go wrong.

We can't always get our way.

Change your perspective.

## CREATE YOURSELF

Those with a bad past.

Can create a bright future.

Design a great one.

## MLK

Can you help others?

Life's most persistent question.

Two lives will be changed.

## MAKE HASTE

Do a kindness now.

Tomorrow may be too late.

You just never know.

## THE RIGHT TOOLS

Things were done to you.

Don't judge yourself by this stick.

Get a new ruler.

## RESURFACE

You have been buried.

But your enemies forgot-

You're a sprouting seed.

## WE GET BY

Replace 'I' with 'We'.

Then illness becomes wellness.

Stronger together.

## SOMETHING'S AFOOT

Had no shoes and cried.

Then I met one with no feet.

Together we smiled.

## DANCE IN THE RAIN

Don't wait out the storm.

Learn how to dance in the rain.

Search for your rainbow.

## **BE THE CHANGE**

To soften hard hearts,

Use kind words and do kind things.

Be the change you want.


## **THAT'S ON THEM**

How are you treated?

If others treat you badly-

That is their problem.


## **STAY THE COURSE**

Choosing happiness.

Even when things are the worst.

Stay the happy course.


## **MANY BATTLES**

Struggle will occur.

Don't ever ever give up.

You keep on fighting.

## LOL

Laughter attracts joy.

It's a miraculous cure.

Find reasons to laugh.


## DEFEND YOUR BELT

You are above those,

Who try pulling you downward.

Keep your hands raised champ.


## THIEF IN THE NIGHT

Do not let your past-

Steal away from your present.

You're valuable.


## HATERS GONNA HATE

Be a source of joy.

Critics and haters complain.

Stand out from this group.

## THE END?

Endings in stories.

Are the start of a new one.

Pick up some new books.

## GOOD BOOKKEEPING

Count all your fortunes.

Now count all of your problems.

Which holds the most weight?

## SWITCH IT UP

Hey, are you happy?

If yes, then you're doing fine.

If no, change something.

## NEW PLAN

Stop saying I wish.

Instead start saying I will.

This gets the job done.

## BLEED RED

Not inferior

Nor are you superior.

We are all human.

## THIS IS YOUR CHANCE

Each second is yours.

It's a chance to change your life.

Don't wait much longer.

## EYES UP FRONT

Don't look behind you.

You are not going that way.

Keep your eyes forward.

## STAND

Stand up for what's right.

Even if standing alone.

Protect moral ground.

## BEST OF THE BEST

The best things in life-

Are not even things at all.

Smile if you know that.

## I.R.L

Your reality.

Doesn't depend on others.

Don't let them crack you.

## CASE OF THE MONDAYS

Ok, it's Monday.

Who says it has to be bad?

Make it a great day.

## RESILIENCY

Some kids are playing.

They've suffered many hardships.

How they do inspire.

## KEEP IT SIMPLE

Life's simplicity.

Why must we complicate it?

Why so serious?

## AYE AYE

Sailing a smooth sea.

Won't make a skilled mariner.

Embrace challenges.

## DO YOU CONSENT?

Without your consent-

No one can belittle you.

Do not permit them.

## ON YOUR FEET

To be walked upon,

You have to be lying down.

Stand up and brush off.

## **STORM ON HORIZON**

The winds of anger.

Dim flames of intelligence.

Control the harsh storms.

## **ANGER RISING**

When anger rises-

Think of the consequences.

Step back and just breathe.

## **STUDY HARD**

People will test you.

First, make sure you come prepared.

You will pass with ease.

## **MY SHINE**

You'll not steal my shine.

You may waste your energy.

You won't take what's mine.

## GIVE THANKS

What seems trivial?

I'm thankful for clean water.

Many don't have it.


## WHAT'S MINE IS YOURS

A small portioned lunch.

Shared with me by a good friend.

Nice to be thought of.


## SURPRISE M'FER

Treat me like I can't.

Maybe I'll show that I won't.

Or, I'll surprise you.


## WATER OFF MY BACK

Check out my feathers.

Some might try to ruffle them.

I just fly away.

## LOOK ME IN THE EYE

Can't see eye to eye-

If looking down on people.

Treat others kindly.

## TAKE AS NEEDED

Here's a remedy.

When you get angry, give pause.

Delay your actions.

## WORLDVIEW

You can change your world.

Change how some things are perceived.

You might feel better.

## RE-APPROACH

Don't like it, change it.

If it's something you can't change,

Change thoughts about it.

## IN TIME

Sadness will occur.

This moment in time shall pass.

Momentarily.

## IN THEIR LIFE

Be there for those there.

Before they're no longer there.

There, I've said my piece.

## REFLECTIONS

Anniversary.

Not really a happy one.

But now I can smile.

## BACK TO LIFE

The season of spring.

Rejuvenation of life.

And so it begins.

## LEARN SOMETHING NEW

My education.

A lifelong journey I'm on.

Never cease to learn.

## HUMAN EMOTION

Angry! Kick! Scream! Cry!

Best not let the beast inside.

Sit back, give it time.

## KEEP IT REAL

Have a little hope.

But keep expectations real.

Keep yourself grounded.

## CAN'T ALWAYS GET WHAT YOU WANT

Having what you want.

This is not true happiness.

Value what you have.

### FALL 7X STAND 8

We fall many times.

Dust yourself off and get up.

Nothing keeps us down.

### FOOTPRINTS

We can glance backwards.

Study the paths we traveled.

New paths await us.

### CHANCES

Failure is your chance.

It's your opportunity.

Learn and start over.

### MAKE IT COUNT

We may live for years.

But how much life did you live?

Make each moment count.

## **LIFE'S JOURNEY**

State of happiness.

It's not a destination.

It's a way of life.

## **A PRESENT**

The past is a dream.

Tomorrow just a vision.

Today is a gift.

## **PRACTICE MAKES PERFECT**

Practice tolerance.

Enemies are great teachers.

Respond with kindness.

## **TWO LAWNS**

The grass is greener-

Where you choose to water it.

Don't compare two lawns.

## **CHOOSE A SIDE**

You have potential.

You can choose to do evil.

Or be a hero.


## **SPRING HAS SPRUNG**

The blossoming trees.

The smell of freshly cut grass.

Life is beautiful.


## **DECENT PRICE**

Happiness is free.

It's not in material.

Put your cash away.


## **ATTITUDE OF GRATITUDE**

Gratitude journal.

Write in it at least daily.

Why are you thankful?

## BATTER'S UP

Life can throw curve balls.

It is a Cy Young winner.

Your bat is mighty.

## SO YOU HAD A BAD DAY

You had a bad day.

What is it that made it so?

Could it have been worse?

## SPACE OUT

A stressful work day.

Time to sit back and relax.

Deep breath in and out.

## SOCIAL NATURE

Love from another.

It's a natural desire.

We're social creatures.

## ALONE TIME

Spend some time alone.

But don't isolate yourself.

Allow others in.

## WHAT YOU'RE MADE OF

Some will build you up.

Some others will break you down.

This is what makes us.

## SYSTEMS OF SUPPORT

Do not suffer shame-

If you need to seek some help.

Embrace your supports.

## MATURE

Act like an adult.

Even when others do not.

Don't sink down with them.

## STAY CALM

Keep calm when tested.

Bravely face your challenges.

If knocked down, get up.

## READY FOR BATTLE

You're a warrior.

You are on life's battlefield.

Swords and shields ready.

## IN THEIR SHOES

Step into their shoes.

Is the fit comfortable?

Make sure your own fit.

## SET YOU FREE

Don't "win" to score points.

Try to "win" in search of truth.

The truth sets us free.

## TEMPTATION

When you are tempted,

To lash out in violence,

Take some slow, deep breaths.


## OPINIONS ARE LIKE…

Our thoughts may differ.

Opinions are quite varied.

Where can we agree?


## LUMPING

Stereotyping.

And generalizations.

Avoid at all costs.


## STAY CURIOUS

Curiosity.

Use instead of assuming.

Seek out your answers.

## SPREAD THE WEALTH

Focus on learning.

Teach others what you have learned.

Freely spread the wealth.

## MIRROR MIRROR

That special someone.

I look to my right and left.

Then, in a mirror.

## START OF THE DAY

A positive thought.

This is how to start your day.

Then, go grab breakfast.

## MISSING

Missing somebody?

Call them or invite them out.

Don't complicate life.

## EYE OF BEHOLDER

Perceiving beauty.

Allow yourself permission.

Be warned! Tears may flow.

## CONVO STARTER

Talking to people.

Not as hard as it may seem.

Hello is step one.

## UNBROKEN

You may feel broken.

But you're not beyond repair.

You're forever strong.

## ON GUARD

The sun will soon rise.

Tomorrow we try again.

Remain vigilant.

## ADJUSTMENT NEEDED

Learn from your mistakes.

We cannot reach perfection.

Correct your errors.

## FAULTY US

We all have our faults.

If you feel you don't have one:

That's one you can add.

## BREAK FREE

Break free from your cage.

Now go and retrieve your crown.

You are royalty.

## VAST FORTUNES

Today I give thanks.

Thankful for many riches.

I'm quite fortunate.

## PUDDLES

Dark skies have emerged.

The storm brings in heavy rains.

Dance in the puddles.


## RARE FLOWER

Beautiful flower.

Don't get plucked for your beauty.

Be rare and grow wild.


## THE BEST OF US

Happens to us all.

Sometimes you need to know this.

You are not alone.


## FREE BIRD

Birds fly with purpose.

Yet, there's freedom in their flight.

This is my life's aim.

## SOAK IT UP

Piles of books to read.

Information to absorb.

Be a data sponge.


## ROLL THE DICE

Feeling uncertain.

Decide to take some chances.

There's one life to live.


## SEE THE WORLD

Destination booked.

I want to travel the world.

Do this while you can.


## YOU'RE THE GATE KEEPER

What thoughts consume you?

These are your reality.

Let the right ones in.

## **BEWARE GREEN-EYED MONSTERS**

Celebrate others.

Don't wallow in jealousy.

Focus on your goals.

## **FALSE NARRATIVE**

You're not good enough.

You have somehow been convinced.

Well, this is bullshit!

## **PASSIONS**

What is your passion?

Follow this path where it leads.

It ends with your joy.

## **STURDY**

My base is stable.

It would be hard to rock me.

I won't be shaken.

## SHACKLED

Victims of our minds.

Don't shackle yourself like this.

No stinking thinking.

## AT THE READY

Relax and prepare.

Your future depends on it.

Readiness is key.

## HAPPY PLACE

Go on adventures.

Discover where you belong.

Happy place awaits.

## SHORT WICK

Our lives are too short.

Love truly and have some fun.

Do what makes you smile.

## HOWL

Been tossed to the wolves.

Became the wolf pack leader.

Listen to my howl.


## INTENTION

Live life with intent.

Act with purpose and speak truth.

Have integrity.


## THAT'S COMEDY?

Seek out some humor.

Find any reason to laugh.

Make others laugh too.


## 'S' ON CHEST

A random, kind act.

It doesn't take much at all.

Be someone's hero.

## TOXINS

Toxic relations.

They block the path to true love.

Remove barriers.

## SINGLE STEP

A long, hard journey.

One that has to be taken.

It must start somewhere.

## LIFE'S WHAT YOU MAKE IT

Pondering meaning.

There are not concrete answers.

Life's what you make it.

## THE LITTLE THINGS

I woke up today.

I had clean clothes to put on.

I had food to eat.

## INTERNAL BEAUTY

Beauty lies within.

How do you perceive yourself?

This is what matters.

## PROVE IT

Things are often said.

But back up the things you say.

Prove what's said is true.

## SPOT ME

Holding heavy weight.

Make sure you have a spotter.

Or, it could all fall.

## I LOVE YOU MOM

Mother's Day comes soon.

I don't need one day a year-

To say, "I love you".

## PRESSURE

Don't bottle it up.

Find an outlet to release.

Try not to explode.


## REMAINS

Let go of what's gone.

Be grateful for what remains.

Live here, in the now.


## GIVE IT A CHANCE

Resistance of change.

This is denial of growth.

You can welcome both.


## DEDICATION

Some dreams can come true.

Not by wishing on a star.

By working for them.

## PRESENT OF PRESENCE

Your very presence.

It's a present to the world.

Present it proudly.

## ONE OF A KIND

You are quite unique.

You're an individual.

Stand out from the crowd.

## MANY FLAVORS

Make life what you want.

Do not limit your options.

Life's full of flavors.

## IN THE NOW

Moment to moment.

Just be present in the now.

Focus on your goal.

## **ROW TOGETHER**

We all face troubles.

You're not alone in this boat.

Face them together.


## **HANDS UP**

Whatever you face.

Stand up to it and be brave.

Hands up at all times.


## **SELF-REFLECTION**

You have the answers.

Many are deep within you.

Take time to reflect.


## **NOBILITY**

Be understanding.

Have courage, strength, self-esteem.

Noble qualities.

## PRO VS. CON

Decision making.

Weigh all possible options.

Proceed with caution.

## MOUNTAIN TOPS

Reach the highest peaks.

Get prepared for the journey.

It's a long, cold trek.

## CHILD'S EYES

Bare feet in the grass.

Bright sun shining on my face.

Like a child at play.

## MOVED

Music can move us.

What direction do you want?

Move at your own pace.

## HAWKEYE

Keep eyes on target.

Take arrow from the quiver.

Pull back and release.

## WASTE

Constant worrying.

Nothing wastes more energy.

Move into the now.

## WHAT DO YOU LIFT?

Carrying problems.

With time they get heavier.

Who can help you lift?

## METAMORPHOSIS

Eat, caterpillar.

Soon you'll be a butterfly.

Prepare for the change.

## DON'T KICK THE DOG

If you are angered-

Don't take it out on loved ones.

Guide your emotions.


## ROLE MODEL

Be a creator.

One who initiates change.

You're a role model.


## EPIC

Behind each person,

There's a story to be told.

Yours should be epic.


## BUSY HANDS

Brain on rapid mode.

Invasive thoughts come and go.

Need to keep busy.

## **SHOW LOVE**

Family comes first.

All else gets pushed to the side.

Show loved ones you care.


## **HEAL OR HURT**

Words can be hurtful.

They have power and meaning.

They can also heal.


## **INDELIBLE**

Make your worldly mark.

Make sure it's indelible.

Soon we'll be erased.


## **ALL YOU NEED IS LOVE**

Promote what you love.

Don't waste energy on hate.

Love is all we need.

## IF YOU WANT IT

Thinking about goals?

Then don't stop working for them.

It will be worth it.

## PRIORITIZE

What you want and need.

Distinguish between the two.

Which should fill your life?

## NURTURED

Planted some veggies.

They'll be cared for and watered.

In time they will grow.

## YIN & YANG

The spider will prey.

The fly becomes entangled.

Both play vital roles.

## WHAT DEFINES YOU

Defining moments.

These have made you who you are.

Be on the lookout.

## LOVE YOURSELF

Love the way you are.

If you want change, then make it.

If not, let it go.

## SCREAM AND SHOUT

Elevate your voice.

Scream for love and honesty.

Shout out against hate.

## NOURISHMENT

Avoid eye candy.

Seek a love who is soul food.

It's more nourishing.

## KEEP SWINGING

Fatigue has set in.

There's still more fight to be fought.

There's no quit in me.


## DISCUSSION

Screaming your viewpoint.

This does not make it valid.

Take time to listen.


## CHEERS

Friends celebrate wins.

Those who celebrate failures?

They are not your friends.


## ROOM TO STRETCH

Your home is your space.

May it be comfortable.

Eliminate junk.

## BEGIN AGAIN

Restart and reset.

Readjust and refocus.

Do so when needed.

## CLEAN UP CLEAN UP..

Clean out all the junk.

Eliminate the excess.

Give to those in need.

## A PIECE OF YOU

Your contribution.

What will be your legacy?

Leave a piece of you.

## THE CATALYST

Execute your moves.

First one is to move yourself.

Then to move the world.

## **CHALLENGE ACCEPTED**

Novelty of life.

Dare to step out of your lane.

Accept challenges.

## **WE'RE ALL FAMILY**

Love one another.

We're all sisters and brothers.

Treat others as such.

## **IN PASSING**

Passing by strangers.

Here is opportunity.

A chance to be kind.

## **CAN'T WIN THEM ALL**

Hey there warrior!

Many battles await you.

Some of them you'll win.

## JOURNAL ENTRY

Took a hot shower.

Drank some clean bottled water.

For this I'm grateful.


## ROCK THE VOTE

I just got to vote.

An incredible feeling.

Some still fight for this.


## HIJACKED

Anger consumes mind.

Rational thought is hijacked.

Rage against this thief.


## INTO THE DARK

Reach into darkness.

Pull the blind into the light.

Bring your own matches.

## SIGHT SEEING

Go on a road trip.

Listen to awesome music.

Take in all the sights.


## YOU GO THIS

You should remember-

There are people who love you.

You WILL get through this.


## BE YOU

No compromises.

Not for self-identity.

Just be who you are.


## PRO-TRUTH PLEDGE

Do not share a lie.

Do not spread any falsehoods.

Do your own research.

## MINDFULNESS

Relax your body.

Clear your mind of harmful thoughts.

Meditate often.


## NO BITCHING

What an awesome day.

Had many chances to bitch.

I remained grateful.


## LANGUAGE OF PAIN

Listen to the pain.

Don't try to shut it away.

Learn from it and grow.


## FLOAT

Anxiety strikes.

Worry about the unknown.

Float away at peace.

## EYES ON PRIZE

Positive outlook.

That's what I'll maintain today.

Keep eyes on the prize.

## STRENGTH FROM PAIN

Pain becomes your strength.

You may not realize it.

Give yourself some time.

## EVICTION NOTICE

Chaos inside you.

Construct a sturdy temple.

Evict intruders.

## FORGED IN FLAMES

Consumed by the fire.

Some crumble into ashes.

Some forged by the flames.

## **FORWARD MARCH**

Took two steps forward.

Was just knocked back a few steps.

Yet I keep marching.


## **CAN'T OUT RUN**

I ran many miles.

Upstairs, down hills, cross-country.

My problems kept pace.


## **CIN CIN**

Worries wash away.

Surrounded by family.

Let's eat, drink, and laugh.


## **FORGIVE ME**

Time for forgiveness.

Forgive yourself and others.

Happiness awaits.

## PRICE TAGS

Where you are today-

There was a price to be paid.

There are no refunds.


## BEGIN WITH A SMILE

Some things war can do-

Peace can do even better.

Begin with a smile.


## OK TO CRY

Take care of yourself.

Let go and cry if needed.

Loved ones embrace you.


## MY WISH FOR YOU

Total happiness.

Joy in everything you do.

This I wish for you.

## PUZZLE

Gather the pieces.

A loss makes us feel shattered.

Collect all of you.


## KEEP LOOKING

Seek and you will find.

Put forth all of your effort.

You'll be rewarded.


## BROADER PICTURE

Focus on the tree-

And you might miss the forest.

A large world awaits.


## GET TO WORK

The day is dragging.

Too focused on going home.

Re-shifting thoughts now.

## MOVE TO A NEW BEAT

Songs on side 'A' end.

Flip the record to side 'B'.

Tap your feet once more.


## SIZE CHART

One size won't fit all.

Examine definitives.

What works best for you?


## POLES

Be so positive-

Negative people take heed.

Changed polarity.


## FIRST AID

Caustic memories.

Corrosive to happiness.

Seek first aid with haste.

## BE

Be kind but not weak.

Be humble but not timid.

Be daring but wise.

## SUNSHINE

Don't create a storm-

And complain about the rain.

Bathe in the sunshine.

## NO TIME LIKE NOW

The rest of your life.

Make it the best of your life.

You can start right now.

## PIVOT AND PARRY

Punches keep coming.

Block and counter all of them.

There are many rounds.

## SHOW'S ON

Each day won't be good.

Bravely show up anyway.

Face difficulties.


## LET THEM TALK

People will gossip.

Go ahead and let them talk.

None of our concern.


## REMEDY

Be true to yourself.

Bad habits contradict goals.

Seek a remedy.


## IT'S YOUR CALL

Ignore what they say.

You're an individual.

You make your own call.

## HOME DÉCOR

Design your own life.

Don't need a decorator.

This is your own house.

## KICK THE TIRES

Look out for the good.

You will encounter road bumps.

You own the best tires.

## SHOULDER SHRUG

Some might not like you.

You may never escape this.

Keep smiling at them.

## THANKS ALWAYS

Attitude of thanks.

Develop this quality.

Be grateful always.

## **DESTINATIONS**

Get where you're going-

By walking from where you've been.

Tighten your laces.

## **NETFLIX AND CHILL**

Rewind button broke.

There's no fast forward option.

Let the movie play.

## **RESULTS MAY VARY**

Some refuse to grow.

Those ones are holding you back.

You'll grow without them.

## **ELEMENTARY**

Demand evidence.

Be critical and wary.

Exercise reason.

## **STRENGTH > WEAKNESS**

Compliment people.

Focus on strength not weakness.

Build up, don't tear down.

## **OLÉ**

Emotional bulls.

Charging red flags of anger.

Turn your horns away.

## **WALK TALL**

You have made progress.

Walk tall and be proud of this.

Keep your head held high.

## **SMALL GESTURES**

Minute sacrifice.

Smallest gesture remembered.

Look for these moments.

## COMPASS

You're not a lost cause.

You're seeking some direction.

Ask a proper guide.


## HARD FOUGHT BATTLES

Some defeats suffered.

Perhaps a battle that's won.

We must march forward.


## THAT'S HOT

Anger's a hot coal.

Don't grab to throw at someone.

You are the one burned.


## LICENSE AND REGISTRATION

They don't control you.

Your emotions are your own.

You choose which to drive.

## IT'S NORMAL

It's fine to get mad.

Process it and then move on.

Holding it does harm.


## BURNT BRIDGES

Be one who forgives.

We too may need it one day.

Do not burn this bridge.


## HOLD ON TO WHAT'S LOVED

To love anything-

Realize it may be lost.

Tightly embrace love.


## MEASURE OF WEALTH

I'm loved by many.

I may not have much money.

With this love I'm rich.

## TRUE DESIRE

Desire for success.

Elevate this over fear.

Take a leap and try.

## NO STINKING THINKING

Make a happy life.

The possibility's there.

It's in your thinking.

## THOUGHT CHECK

Quality of thought.

This determines your outlook.

How's your current view?

## THEY'LL BE THERE

Don't save any spots-

For those who show no effort.

Loved ones will arrive.

## INDIVIDUALISM

Live your life your way.

Be an individual.

You know who you are.


## ENDURE THE RAIN

Rainbows are present.

After putting up with rain.

Grab an umbrella.


## ROUTINE BREAKER

Take a little trip.

Escape day to day routine.

Discover new worlds.


## LOVE THYSELF

Our first and last love.

It is the love of oneself.

We must work at this.

## MANY DOORS

Doors will close on you.

Some to be locked forever.

Quit banging on them.

## BEFORE YOU ACT

Free to make choices.

We're not free from consequence.

Think before acting.

## IN NEED

This is what friends do.

They show up when you need them.

Who's in your corner?

## WITHERED

Water your garden.

Your responsibility.

Don't let plants wither.

## FUGAZEE

Own expensive clothes.

Own and drive the fastest cars.

Do not own fake friends.

## TIME MANAGEMENT

Laughing at humor.

Dancing to some great music.

Don't be distracted.

## REACH

You have felt struggle.

Reach out for warm, helping hands.

They will lift you up.

## THIS WAY PLEASE

I started the fire.

Not one of devastation.

One to light the way.

## EFFORT

Secrets to success.

None of them will really work.

Unless you work, too.


## IT'S A WONDERFUL LIFE

A wonderful life.

Moments that leave you breathless.

May you have many.


## YOU ARE THE WORLD

To the world you're one.

To one, you may mean the world.

You are their safe place.


## BETTER DAYS

You've seen better days.

Perhaps you've also seen worse.

Next stop, tomorrow.

## CONCEALED

Velvet gloves caress.

Can conceal an iron fist.

Careful shaking hands.

## LET THERE BE LIGHT

The blinds closed tightly.

A beautiful day outside.

Let some light enter.

## GOOSFRABA

Whirlwinds in your head.

Thoughts flying out of control.

You can calm the storm.

## MY TAKE

My philosophy:

Do good and be productive.

This is life's meaning.

## GRAB A SPOON

Life's a bowl of soup.

You think you have only forks.

But spoons surround you.


## $HIT HAPPENS

Don't beg them to stay.

Unwanted goodbyes happen.

This can be a gift.


## BEHIND THE CLOUDS

Dark skies form above.

Soaking rain pours from the clouds.

The sun is still there.


## RISE ABOVE

Rise above nonsense.

Don't get angry or enraged.

Keep your light shining.

## FLEETING

Make some memories.

Take every chance you can get.

Our lives are fleeting.

## ALL OF ME

I want to create.

All that is me will go on.

Won't be forgotten.

## THE HAUNTING

Say what you mean to.

Mean everything that you say.

Your words can haunt you.

## TOGETHER WE CAN

Let us all make change.

Let's hope to be successful.

Let's do it as one.

## ADAPTATION

Improvise. Adapt.

Overcome your obstacles.

Be and do your best.


## ENVIRONMENTALIST

Flower doesn't bloom.

Tend to its environment.

Don't change the flower.


## WIN-WIN

Less fortunate plight.

Reach down to help pull them up.

This is a win-win.


## TO DISAGREE

Try civility.

You may not always agree.

Discuss with kindness.

## **GAME CHANGER**

Be a game changer.

Change the game for those in need.

Ready player one?


## **DIVIDENDS**

Invest in friendships.

These buy- ins are bull markets.

Always a smart move.


## **MADE OF STAR STUFF**

We are all special.

We are all made of star stuff.

Gaze up in wonder.


## **EYE LEAK**

Go ahead and cry.

Give yourself the permission.

Sometimes we need to.

## GO

You can sit and sulk.

You can let your thoughts hinder.

Or, get up and move.


## INVALUABLE

You are solid gold.

A jewel shining brightly.

Maintain that polish.


## NICE PLACE TO VISIT

Living in the past.

Is dying in the present.

Visit and then leave.


## MEMORY MAKER

Unforgettable.

Jump in the pool fully clothed.

Unpredictable.

## SHIFT

Change your perception.

This must come from within you.

No one can force it.

## THROUGH THE PAIN

Just keep on going.

No matter how much you've cried.

You keep on moving.

## RADIATE

Radiate kindness.

Those around you will feel it.

May it penetrate.

## TENACITY

Have tenacity.

This is C.P.R for hope.

Try, try, try again.

## CAN YOU DIG IT?

You possess shovels.

But stop digging your own grave.

Instead plant flowers.


## SCANNERS

Be intentional.

Notice your space this moment.

Scan your surroundings.


## NOW OPEN

Always be humble.

Open to new ideas.

Show humility.


## DOUSERS OF JOY

Feed the flames of joy.

Fan the fires of happiness.

Beware the sprinklers.

## DARE TO EXPLORE

Enter the dark cave.

It may have treasure you seek.

Don't fear to explore.

## FAMILY CHOICE

Can't choose family?

I think that's inaccurate.

But choose them wisely.

## FREE AT LAST

Don't dwell in your cave.

Dare to step into the light.

Unshackle your bonds.

## FORTRESS OF SOLITUDE

Escape from the noise.

Seek silence and solitude.

Put your mind at ease.

## WOKE

Awaken wonder.

Stir your curiosity.

Discover new worlds.

## ROOTS

With strong roots trees thrive.

Strangle them and they wither.

Take care of your roots.

## ZONE DEFENSE

Take a few chances.

Roam outside your comfort zone.

Dare to have some fun.

## ASK FOR DIRECTIONS

It is your own life.

You must travel your own path.

Accept some guidance.

## NO RESERVATION REQUIRED

Find a recipe.

Prepare a decent dinner.

Dine with family.


## PEACEFUL RESISTANCE

Stand for your beliefs.

Even if that means kneeling.

Make your voice be heard.


## ASPIRATION

Aspire to inspire

It will not go unnoticed.

Most of all by you.


## BIT ROLE

Playing a small role.

A part of something larger.

You can be the change.

## KEEP CLIMBING

Still some way to go.

We shall climb even higher.

One slip won't deter.


## SURFACED

You're a survivor.

You surface from ocean depths.

A Phoenix from ash.


## GIVE FREELY

Be charitable.

Give what you can when you can.

You'll feel good you did.


## OFF A DUCK'S BACK

You can obtain peace.

Shrug off what you can't control.

Learn to walk away.

## MANY PATHS

You traveled a path.

Know that more paths lie ahead.

You are not stuck here.


## STOP TRIPPIN'

You're tripping on thoughts.

Be alert, step over them.

Brush off dirty hands.


## BATTLE'S JUST BEGUN

Don't give up or in.

Give everything that you've got.

Put down that white flag.


## A ROUND OF KINDNESS

Kindness is not hard.

It won't cost you all that much.

Spread it all around.

## LOVE REMAINS

People will screw up.

Me, you, and all your loved ones.

Don't remove your love.


## ACTIVE LISTENING

Be silent, listen.

Two words with the same letters.

Interesting, no?


## ARCHITECTURE

Don't fear a fresh start.

Build something new and better.

You're the architect.


## SORROW'S SEA

Sail through sorrow's sea.

Raise the mast of happiness.

Better shores ahead.

## **LOVE IS LOVE**

Loved for who you are.

Loved unconditionally.

Love is love is love.

## **WE MUST NEVER GIVE UP**

Don't give up on life.

Nourish it with hope and love.

Put forth the effort.

## **GO FORTH**

This day's a struggle.

An uphill battle ahead.

We keep it moving.

## **TIME**

Time waits for no one.

It won't slow down or speed up.

Manage yours wisely.

## PONDERINGS

Awareness is key.

It is said to know thyself.

Take time to do so.

## STABBED

Dagger to the heart.

Seek emotional doctors.

The bleeding will clot.

## WATCH YOUR TONGUE

Good first impressions.

Try to think before you speak.

You might gain new friends.

## MOVE MAKER

Start to self-reflect.

Are you where you want to be?

If not, make some moves.

## LOVE ME TENDER

Evolve beyond hate.

It consumes our happiness.

Love with tenderness.

## MOUNTAINS

Mountains on your back.

The enormous weight crushes.

They're meant to be climbed.

## GREATNESS

That which you can give.

This determines your greatness.

Not the things you have.

## TOURISTS

Land of happiness.

There's no permanent housing.

But visit often.

## WANDERER

Seek education.

We should always be learning.

Keep your mind busy.

## BALANCE

There's expectations.

Then there is reality.

Keep the two balanced.

## STURDY BRIDGES

Cross sturdy bridges.

When raging water rises.

Watch the stream below.

## CLEARER VIEW

Trim back your hedges.

Your view of the world is blocked.

And we can't see you.

## MINDSET

Don't rely on "them".

Your happiness starts with you.

It's about mindset.

## YOU TIME

Quiet solitude.

Take the time to play catch up.

Or enjoy silence.

## MENDING

To those you have wronged-

Seek and ask for forgiveness.

Mend relationships.

## ENJOY THE RIDE

Life is turbulent.

There are some bumps; ups, and downs.

Sit back and enjoy.

## CAPE NOT NEEDED

Be someone's hero.

No need for capes or lassos.

Just a small, kind deed.


## HEALING PROCESS

Sustained pain subsides.

Be sure to help yourself heal.

You're worthy of that.


## MODELING

Words may not mean much,

If actions do not follow.

Be that role model.


## WHY SO SERIOUS?

Do not stress too much.

There's nothing that's permanent.

This thing too shall pass.

## EMBRACE THE DAY

The sun shines on you.

Come out from behind shadows.

Embrace the day's warmth.

## ON DISPLAY

Unbound potential.

Don't let talents go to waste.

Show them off proudly.

## CURATOR

Curate your own life.

Be discerning in choices.

Your life's on display.

## THEY SHALL COME

Do not chase people.

Be someone who attracts them.

Bees to sweet nectar.

## BURN OUT

You're feeling burned out.

Take some time to meditate.

Then, soldier onward.

## FORTUNATE ONE

If you're reading this,

Consider yourself lucky.

Many reasons why.

## TEAM PLAYERS

You know you're struggling.

There's spectators and players.

Look to your teammates.

## RULES? WHAT RULES?

Cheers to game changers.

Keep trying to change the game.

Some rules need breaking.

## FRUIT LOOP AMONG CHEERIOS

Described a "weirdo".

Different, odd-ball, a freak.

Be your own person.


## PACE YOURSELF

Your speed does not count.

Moving forward is progress.

Go at your own pace.


## HOME PLATE

Feelings of relief.

Brought on by apologies.

Step up to the plate.


## JUST DO IT

Walk barefoot on sand.

Roll around in Spring flowers.

Be in the moment.

## ABOUT TIME

Don't run out of time.

Say it before it's too late.

Seconds tick away.

## ROAD BLOCKS

Have integrity.

Do what is right and truthful.

There will be road blocks.

## GREAT IMPACT

Give thanks for small things.

Shelter, clean clothes, a warm meal.

Small but meaningful.

## HAVE A SIP

You are the vessel.

You contain cheer, hope, and love.

Let the thirsty drink.

## **MOTHS TO A FLAME**

They can't steal your shine.

Keep your fire burning brightly.

Your warmth draws them in.


## **HOLD ON TO HOPE**

When hope is all gone,

Time can be a punishment.

Hold tightly to hope.


## **WHEN DROWNING**

Don't drown in despair.

Grab the thrown life preservers.

Swim towards dry land.


## **TIGHT GRIP**

Learn to let them go.

Don't let it steal inner peace.

Loosen your tight grip.

## FLAWLESS VICTORY

Don't count yourself short.

Believe and you can achieve.

Victory is yours.

## TREATMENT

Treat your open wounds.

If not, infection sets in.

Same goes for trauma.

## YOU DON'T SAY

Keep your ears open.

There's always something to learn.

You don't know it all.

## PUZZLE PIECE

Give a part of you.

A small piece helps build others.

Complete the puzzle.

## TRUE VALUE

You may know the cost.

But do you know the value?

These are not the same.

## ROLL WITH IT

Bad situations.

Many will enter your life.

Roll with the punches.

## HERE'S TO YOU

Raise your glasses high.

Celebrate to the fullest.

Toast to your fortunes.

## DIVE IN

Wade along the shores.

Swim in the deepest oceans.

Either way, get wet.

## CAUSE NO HARM

Practice your restraint.

Hold back your punches and tongue.

Don't cause harm or pain.


## HERE AND NOW

The here and the now.

This is your time to focus.

Don't get distracted.


## LOOK AT THIS PHOTOGRAPH

Say I love you now.

You can't hug a photograph.

Tomorrow's too late.


## THE JONESES

Who are the Joneses?

Why should we keep up with them?

Just do your own thing.

## SPIN

Change your perspective.

Look for a positive spin.

Make the best of it.

## POWER POSSESSION

Difficult people.

Difficult situations.

Give them no power.

## DON'T GO BACK

Promises you make.

Promises are made to keep.

Live by your own word.

## FIGHT FOR WHAT YOU LOVE

Feel like giving up?

This accomplishes nothing.

Fight for all you love.

## OLIVE BRANCH

Do what's difficult.

Extend foes an olive branch.

Gain another friend.


## KEEP DRIVING

Some challenging roads.

Have pretty destinations.

Your ride's not over.


## THE RIGHT TOOL

Wrench thrown in the works.

Nothing is going as planned.

Pick up your toolbox.


## WISDOM

Please be forgiving.

Also be understanding.

But don't be foolish.

## ESCAPE

Seek your escape route.

Avoid the toxins in life.

Don your masks and shields.

## A NEW DAY

The sun sets each day.

End of one starts another.

A fresh beginning.

## CHARGE YOUR BATTERIES

Days doing nothing.

Sometimes that is all we need.

Let yourself recharge.

## LONG ROAD AHEAD

Arduous journeys.

Must make the initial step.

Keep looking forward.

## SCARS TELL STORIES

Bandage open wounds.

Allow to heal with some time.

Scars are reminders.


## DARWIN KNOWS BEST

Keep on evolving.

Adjust your views if needed.

Disown stubbornness.


## SECRET KINDNESS

A secret kindness.

Do as many as you can.

Be the catalyst.


## CHESS MOVES

Slide pawns into place.

Reflect upon your next move.

Exercise caution.

## **MORALS OVER MONEY**

Dollar signs cloud minds.

Place morals above money.

Some things can't be bought.

## **ADVENTUROUS**

Adventure awaits.

It's right outside the front door.

There's no time like now.

## **NOVELTY**

Be spontaneous.

Dare to do something novel.

Create memories.

## **BUCKET FULL**

Fill up your bucket.

Carry kindness, love, respect.

Toss burdens of hate.

## STAND OUT

Uniformity.

Nothing could be more boring.

Stand out from the crowd.


## RESIST

Laws of injustice.

We must resist and oppose.

Morals can't be bought.


## BE OPEN

The love of your life.

May you one day discover.

Always be looking.


## LEGACY

One day you'll be gone.

How will we remember you?

What will you leave us?

## A SIMPLE 'THANK YOU'

Appreciation.

Extend to those deserving.

Let them know you care.

## COMMON GROUND

Bitterness repels.

Anger held causes distance.

Find some common ground.

## SERENITY NOW

Seek serenity.

Don't let chaos penetrate.

Sport your calmness cloak.

## NEVER ALONE

You're never alone.

Surround yourself with loved ones.

Don't self-isolate.

## **TAKE IN THE BEAUTY**

Lives hurried and rushed.

You miss the beauty nearby.

Take some time to look.

## **MINIMIZE LIMITS**

Don't waste any time.

Make sure to do what you love.

Minimize limits.

## **SQUANDERED**

Limited in time.

Don't allow it to squander.

Please use yours wisely.

## **SET REAL GOALS**

Achievable goals.

Set up real expectations.

Then work towards them.

## TRACTION

We may often slip.

But we can regain traction.

Always stand back up.


## RARE COMMODITY

More precious than gold.

A true rare commodity.

Never forget that.


## FRACTURED

Trauma can fracture.

Love and beauty are healers.

Take time to know them.


## COME SAIL AWAY

Harbor ships are safe.

But that's not why ships are built.

Explore open seas.

## IN FLOW

Bad days won't change me.

Negative people either.

I'll stay in my flow.


## EXPLORE

Don't like where you are.

And not where you used to be.

Your path continues.


## TIGGER

A spring in your step.

Bounce around just like Tigger.

It is infectious.


## MEET YOUR GOALS

Falling from habits.

Must now rise to meet your goals.

It's a worthwhile fight.

## TERMS

Your peace has been sold.

This cost is too expensive.

Revisit the terms.

## ALTERED

We alter our life-

By altering our thinking.

What change will you make?

## SMILES AT US ALL

That eternal sleep.

It comes for each one of us.

No sense worrying.

## THERE WILL BE BAD DAYS

Regression occurs.

You can still take forward steps.

There will be bad days.

## CREATE

Art's a form of love.

It's an expression of self.

It's a piece of you.


## AGE OF REASON

The age of reason.

We have fought hard to get here.

Let us not revert.


## STAR BRIGHT

The brightest of stars.

You light up the darkest skies.

Keep showing the way.


## YOU'RE A TEMPLE

Foundation crumbling.

Pick up pieces and rebuild.

Strengthen your temple.

## BON VOYAGE

A map and a plan.

Set out on a new voyage.

Be bold and be brave.


## RUNG BELL

Bells can't be un-rung.

Hateful words can leave imprints.

Think before you speak.


## SCRUB

Stains will make their mark.

Elbow grease can help remove.

Hard work is required.


## TURN, TURN, TURN

Changes will take place.

Often they are not easy.

The strong will adapt.

## FILL'ER UP

Tank's almost empty.

Currently running on fumes.

Both hands on the wheel.


## DECREASE DISTANCE

Care in your approach.

Do not keep loved ones distant.

Civility works.


## CONTEMPLATION

Impulsive choices.

Decisions made way too soon.

Give yourself some time.


## STUDY SESSION

People will test you.

Do the best that you can do.

Cram for your finals.

## **CELEBRATE LIFE**

Celebrating life.

Don't need yearly excuses.

Toast and cheers often.

## **GROUNDED**

Mountains seem too big.

Start out by climbing some hills.

Keep yourself grounded.

## **SLOW & STEADY**

Try when you're ready.

The mountain will still be there.

Go at your own pace.

## **DAY OF REST**

Rest is not defeat.

A day's not eternity.

Allow yourself time.

## RAYS BREAK THROUGH

Heavy fog will lift.

We need a little sunshine.

Hold on for the rays.


## POTHOLES

A rough road ahead.

Keep eyes open for potholes.

Travel forth slowly.


## ONE STEP AT A TIME

Give a little bit.

Take baby steps every day.

You will reach your goal.


## SHIP'S CREW

Steady as she goes.

Maintain your course in calm seas.

Your crew's there for storms.

## CHILD'S EYES

The world through child's eyes.

Be curious about all.

A new, stress free view.

## RIGHT AMOUNT OF CRAZY

Sprawled out in the dirt.

Face up catching the raindrops.

Dressed in my finest.

## MINOR DEVIATION

Escape your routine.

Deviate from the normal.

Taste other flavors.

## CHARGING STATIONS

Motivation gone.

Find inspirational guides.

Get moving again.

## YOU GOT THIS

Improvement takes time.

The process can be painful.

Know that you got this.

## STAGNATION

Your life's stagnation.

Past time to make some new moves.

There's no time like now.

## STORY OF YOU

The story of you.

What do you want to be read?

Who's your narrator?

## CLOSE ENCOUNTERS

Parallel pathways.

Different but worthwhile goals.

Stay within arm's length.

## ATTEND TO THIS

Hey, YOU reading this!

Can I have your attention?

Thanks for focusing.

## ROAD WELL-TRAVELED

The road ahead worn.

It's been traveled many times.

Seek out directions.

## TEMP STATUS

Nothing gold can stay.

No cluttering garbage should.

All's temporary.

## OK SHERLOCK

Wonder then wisdom.

Be curious and seek truth.

Be like Sherlock Holmes.

## GUT PUNCH

Love found and then lost.

Gut punch that leaves you gasping.

Take time to catch breath.

## ROUTINELY

Find your own routine.

Dedicate your time to it.

Results will follow.

## DON'T BE DISCOURAGED

Discouraged today.

Discouraged tomorrow too.

Don't give up the fight.

## WASTED

Your time and talents.

Two things that you should not waste.

Share them with the world.

## ILLUMINATION

Light of unity.

It illuminates the world.

Bear and share this torch.

## SAND THROUGH THE HOURGLASS

Don't waste time waiting.

Not as much time as you think.

Do or say it now.

## AVOID ASSUMPTIONS

Assumptions are made.

Making an ass out of you.

Makes one of me too.

## CARRY ON

Great people pass on.

We carry their legacy.

Start building your own.

## OK TO FAIL

Well, at least I tried.

More than some others can say.

Try, fail, try again.


## NOTHING VENTURED

Venture on your own.

Don't fear going it alone.

Get your feet moving.


## BLUEPRINTS

You're the architect.

It's of your dreams or demise.

Construct your future.


## PASSAGE OF PAIN

Pain will come and go.

But I welcome its passage.

It shows I'm alive.

## CONTEMPT

Answering contempt.

Respond with warm heartedness.

This displays real strength.

## REBEL YELL

Lead the rebellion.

Obtain peace and harmony.

This change starts with you.

## HAVES & NOTS

Aching for have nots.

Be joyous for all the haves.

Changed thoughts change your world.

## DENIED PRIVILEGE

Don't regret aging.

Some denied this privilege.

Enjoy the journey.

## JUST SAY NO

Learn how to say no.

Don't let others walk on you.

Stand up for yourself.


## NO PLACE LIKE HOME

Home is not a place.

It's wherever loved ones are.

Arms embracing you.


## STOICALLY

Stare down your problems.

Face them with a Stoic air.

Find your calm, then solve.


## PASSIVE OBSERVER

Sit back and observe.

Don't always have to react.

Study your next move.

## SEEDLING

We're all but seedlings.

Relationships help us sprout.

Grow as we're nourished.

## LOST IN THE MOMENT

Lost in what you love.

Your time is never wasted.

Do prioritize.

## HERE COMES THE FUNK

In some sort of funk.

Exercise is your best friend.

Got to keep moving.

## RISEN

You've been through descent.

Now let them all watch you rise.

The stage is now yours.

## STRAY

Push the boundaries.

Don't fear trying something new.

Divert from routine.

## ON THE OUTSIDE

Creativity.

Color outside of the lines.

Think outside the box.

## EYES PEELED

Hope is never lost.

Just have to know where to look.

Keep your eyes open.

## WHO'S IN CHARGE?

They'll do what they do.

You're only in charge of you.

Others just the guides.

## ONLY MAKE BELIEVE

Part-time pretend friends.

Their selfish measures are drains.

Maintain your distance.

## TEAR DOWN THESE WALLS

Attempt compromise.

Don't let bitterness divide.

Tear down barriers.

## CYCLICAL DISDAIN

Words of gratitude.

Can break cyclical disdain.

Speak kindly with love.

## PANTS ON FIRE

Anxiety lies.

Your brain's trying to trick you.

Pay close attention.

## PILOT

Your time is flying.

Good news is you're the pilot.

Which way will you go?

## MAKE TIME

Never too busy.

You are important enough.

I'll come when you call.

## PAL

Holding resentment.

It's as corrosive as hate.

Maintain peace and love.

## CHIP

Hold a sturdy grip.

Visualize the end goal.

Keep chipping away.

## HOARDER

Accumulation.

Gather less materials.

Hoard endearing traits.

## AT THE READY

There's good and bad news.

Much can change within a year.

Shields at the ready.

## FRESH START

Re-set and re-start.

Do as often as needed.

Each day a fresh start.

## SCARED

It's fine to be scared.

Be bold and face your problems.

Stand up and be brave.

## BY EXAMPLE

Initiative.

If it needs done then do it.

Leaders take the lead.

## FIRE AWAY

Your goal's a long shot.

Point, aim, then fire anyway.

Yours to win or lose.

## HEAD ON

Feeling accomplished.

The pride that you give yourself.

Tackle list of goals.

## RAGING ELEPHANTS

Pachyderms of rage.

Defeat logical riders.

See the forest's trees.

## AT FIRST YOU DON'T SUCCEED

Take many first steps.

Maybe take seconds and thirds.

Just don't stop walking.


## STAGE IS YOURS

You're too important.

This world and loved ones need you.

Show us what you've got.


## DEAD END

Many roads ahead.

Choose wisely the path followed.

Some are just dead ends.


## BE PREPARED

You can't calm the storm.

Instead change how you respond.

The storm will soon pass.

## EATING PUNCHES

Life has knocked you down.

Calmly get back up and say:

"You hit like a bitch".


## IT'S JUST MATH

Opposites attract.

Positive moods can decline.

Subtract negatives.


## NAME CALLING

You know what you are?!

Loved, strong, worthy, and needed.

You will be ok.


## HECTIC

Life can get hectic.

Adopt wise time management.

There's no going back.

## **HOLD ON TIGHT**

Beauty of the day.

Bright sun shining upon you.

Don't let it escape.

## **CHEERING YOU ON**

You're trying to heal.

I'm rooting in your corner.

Don't quit on me now.

## **THE ARROGANT**

Ugly arrogance.

No head above, none below.

Keep yourself humble.

## **EXPERIENCE TEACHES**

Making good judgements.

This comes from experience.

Learn from bad judgements.

## VIBE

You're overthinking.

Get back into your flow state.

Eliminate stress.


## OLD YOU IS GONE

You're not what once was.

You're working at what will be.

You're not your mistakes.


## TRAMPLED

Step on a flower?

Given time, it will grow back.

You can do the same.


## LITTLE BLUE DOT

Beautiful blue dot.

You're our one and only home.

Let's treat her that way.

## CIRCUS

Clowns will act like clowns.

Stay away from the circus.

Do not get drawn in.

## EXAMPLE SETTER

Be a role model.

Children see and children do.

Set good examples.

## THAT'S ON THEM

Some might not like you.

Some jealous of your success.

And this is ok.

## YEAH! SCIENCE!

Force yourself to smile.

Brain's happy centers light up.

It's only science.

## SQUATTERS

People in your head.

Squatting unpermitted space.

Time for eviction.

## TAKE IT ALL IN

Accept compliments.

Lend your ears to the critics.

Both help you to bloom.

## BUILD YOUR LIBRARY

Surrounded by books.

So much in this world to learn.

Soak in what you can.

## GONE MOMENT GONE

Treasure each moment.

Each one is so very rare.

When they're gone they're gone.

## WHY WAIT?

Procrastination.

The number one dream killer.

There's no time like now.

## UP & OVER

Things stand in your way.

The obstacles are the path.

March through and over.

## SERENITY

Find a quiet place.

Dwell on the serenity.

Let your mind wander.

## SMILE FOR ME

Joy for little things.

You don't need the world to smile.

The world needs your smile.

## **LOOK OF DETERMINATION**

Determination.

That is the key to success.

The struggle's worth it.

## **ABLAZE**

The fire's in your eyes.

Know what you want and get it.

No one can stop you.

## **LOCKED UP**

Break free from prison.

The prison of our own minds.

We even have keys.

## **IT'S WITHIN**

Worth is internal.

Weight, race, or gender are moot.

Learn to love yourself.

## **STUCK**

Saw this episode.

Already watched this movie.

Veer to the unknown.

## **FREE FALL**

The loss of control.

Sometimes it's out of our hands.

It can be freeing.

## **PRICE**

Don't do it for praise.

You might not get a thank you.

Kindness its own prize.

## **SOLES**

You walk your own path.

Others walk with and guide you.

But none in your shoes.

## UP ON HIGH

You have succeeded.

Recognize all your hard work.

Hold your head up high.

## HABITUAL

One small decision.

Paves the way for our habits.

Work towards good ones.

## LOOSENED GRIP

Ok to let go.

Why hold on to what's toxic?

Follow paths of peace.

## THIS LIFE

Get into this life.

It's the only one you get.

Enjoy while you can.

## WHY ASK WHY

Why did this happen?!

Sometimes you just cannot know.

Don't let it steal bliss.

## MARATHON

Finish line in sight.

Pouring sweat and aching legs.

Crowd's cheering for you.

## WHAT LIES AHEAD

This day's behind you.

The good and bad both have passed.

Tomorrow's coming.

## VICTORY IS YOURS

Smallest victories.

Take them when you can find them.

They will all add up.

## EMPHASIS

Emphasize likeness.

We share commonalities.

Embrace difference.

## PERSPECTIVE

Dandelion fields.

Some will see large plains of weeds.

Some, endless wishes.

## DISTINCTION

Trying to fit in?

It's not always the best thing.

Stand out from the pack.

## OFFERINGS

Something to offer.

You have what someone else needs.

Don't take that away.

## IMMERSED IN PURPOSE

To compare distracts.

Immerse yourself with purpose.

Stay captivated.

## THE HUMANITY

Extend open hands.

Work on solidarity.

All of us bleed red.

## STANDING 8 COUNT

You're incredible.

There may be times you feel weak.

You're not defeated.

## FIRST AND GOAL

Life's always changing.

It won't always be easy.

Tackle it head on.

## KEEP CHURNING

Sacrifices made.

Keep the outcome in your sight.

Make sure it's worthwhile.


## STORM BREAKER

Some storms could break you.

Hunker down in safe shelter.

Emerge to rainbows.


## NOT DONE YET

Fatigue setting in.

But there's so much more to do.

Keep chipping away.


## DEFLECTED

Feeling rejected?

You're only redirected.

A new road ahead.

## **DIRECTIONS**

Where to go from here.

The answer's always forward.

There's more to be done.

## **FAULTS AND FLAWS**

Nobody's perfect.

We all have our faults and flaws.

But we do our best.

## **AW SHUCKS!**

The world's your oyster.

You will find pearls if you look.

Time to start shucking.

## **ALONE IN THE MOONLIGHT**

Cherish the time had.

Create tons of memories.

Look back with a smile.

## **CORNER MEN**

Company we keep.

It can reflect upon us.

Who's in your corner?

## **BOOK COVERS**

Outward appearance.

Can often be deceiving.

Get to know people.

## **C.E.O**

You're the C.E.O.

Fire, hire, and promote people.

Boss of your own life.

## **3 CHEEERS!**

Voice encouragement.

Keep going, you can do it!

That's how it is done.

## **NICENESS COUNTS**

Some people cruel.

Nasty, mean, jealous, hateful.

Don't be one of them.

## **ALL SIDES**

Time to sit and think.

Reflect on all that matters.

Consider all sides.

## **REACH**

Reach out to strangers.

Lend a needed helping hand.

Or just say hello.

## **HEAR THEM OUT**

People go through shit.

We might not know their story.

Take time to listen.

## DISTRACTION

Put down your cellphone.

Just enjoy the atmosphere.

Limit distractions.

## HAND IN HAND

We'll walk together.

Part of our journey's the end.

Make the best of it.

## DEMONS WITHIN

Seek and find your strength.

Conquer the demons within.

You hold the power.

## TAKE 5

Provide some self-care.

You are carrying burdens.

Stop and rest awhile.

## ASK

If you need help, ask.

This can take courage and strength.

Give people the chance.


## WOUNDS

Heal pain of the past.

If not, bleed on your future.

Closure's within you.


## HOLD OR FOLD

What are you holding?

Does it lift up or hold down?

What's your direction?


## ART GALLERY

True colors revealed.

Don't waste your time re-painting.

Admire some new art.

## **TAKE A BREATHER**

Frustration building.

Take some steps back to observe.

Approach when ready.

## **OK TO CRY**

There are times we cry.

Don't believe this is weakness.

It's being human.

## **ONE DAY**

The pain goes away.

It may not leave tomorrow.

But it will one day.

## **DETOUR**

Detoured road ahead.

A sudden shift in the norm.

New path but same goal.

## PROMISES PROMISES

Stay true to your word.

Follow through on promises.

Be reliable.

## JAILBREAK

Shackled in self-doubt.

Try breaking free of confines.

Dare to take a chance.

## DEAR YOU

A note to yourself.

You're capable of greatness.

You're more than enough.

## IT'S ALL AROUND YOU

Inspiration strikes.

Anytime and anywhere.

Pay close attention.

## SIGNS OF LOVE

Saying "I love you".

It's not always done with words.

Show that you love them.


## ADMISSIONS

Admit when you're wrong.

It's the only way you'll grow.

Why limit your growth?


## WALK THIS WAY

Choose to walk away.

This won't always be easy.

But it's for the best.


## HELP WANTED

We may all need help.

Remember, you're not broken.

We just need guidance.

## **BUNTING**

Swing for the fences.

You are a power player.

But a bunt may do.


## **HORSE PILLS**

Hard pills to swallow.

The truth may end up hurting.

Drink tons of water.


## **BORROWED STRENGTH**

Lend someone your strength.

Don't point out perceived weakness.

This defines kindness.


## **MONSTERS**

Some create monsters.

Then say, "Look under my bed".

They must face this beast.

## MOUNTAIN PEAKS

Mountain formation.

By violent collisions.

You too shall soon rise.


## PANIC

When panic attacks.

Concentrate on your breathing.

In and out slowly.


## THRILL SEEKER

Be willing to jump.

To do so might be scary.

Exhilarating.


## HIDDEN TALENTS

You are talented.

Your skills might be in hiding.

But you will find them.

## BE THE CHANGE

You can change the world.

The power is within you.

The world is waiting.


## MOSAIC

Mosaic artwork.

Made of small broken pieces.

Sometimes we are, too.


## SITUATIONAL

Make the best of it.

Presented a shitty deal.

Your fertilizer.


## NOW BATTING

Accidents happen.

Make whole all who have been wronged.

Step up to the plate.

## DEFENDERS OF TRUTH

Not the enemy.

Don't present yourself as such.

Just defend the truth.

## WORDS MATTER

Tell yourself you're 'this'.

Say to yourself you are 'that'.

It's what you'll become.

## GRAB YOUR PADDLES

You've made poor choices.

You're not in that boat alone.

Now to start rowing.

## CONTENDER

This was a rough day.

But you are a tough person.

Tomorrow's round two.

## STATUS

Life's temporary.

Work towards its betterment.

For you and for all.

## TRAIT DEVELOPMENT

Strength of character.

Love, honesty, and kindness.

Develop these traits.

## TIME WELL SPENT

Pulled into nonsense.

Misery loves company.

Spend your time elsewhere.

## WORK TO BE DONE

Strive to be better.

Always room for improvement.

There's work to be done.

## BRIDGE CROSSED

What were you thinking?

Impulsive decision made.

Now change it or deal.


## SUNFLOWER

Roses all around.

Their beauty attracts- thorns pierce.

Be a sunflower.


## BRING IT ON

Your contribution.

What do you bring to the game?

Bring all that you've got.


## EXTRA EXTRA

Unnecessary.

Cut out all of the extra.

You don't need the stress.

## CURIOSITY VOYAGE

Oceans of knowledge.

Curiosity voyage.

Now full steam ahead.

## THE REAL YOU

No need to pretend.

Present to all the real you.

Take it or leave it.

## CLEAN RUGS

You've stepped in some shit.

Don't drag it into the house.

Leave that mess outside.

## SHARKS

The sharks are circling.

Blood and fear is what they smell.

Head's above water.

## ADDITION

Little things add up.

They are all small 'I love yous'.

Notice and give them.


## GRAVITY

You think you're failing.

Some burdens just too heavy.

Who will help you lift?


## PROS & CONS

Weigh the pros and cons.

What works out the best for you?

That's what you should do.


## PUZZLED

We fall to pieces.

Enter great puzzle solvers.

Keep them by your side.

## **OBJECTS IN MOTION**

Recognized problem.

What's the corrective action?

Set into motion.

## **MELT**

Be silent, be still.

Take note of your surroundings.

Let stress melt away.

## **NO PLACE LIKE IT**

Spend some time away.

It will provide an escape.

But home's where hearts thrive.

## **DAYS OF OUR LIFE**

This right here is it.

We have one life and one chance.

Will you make it count?

## VAST WORLD

So much world to see.

Experiences await.

Enjoy its beauty.


## ANYTHING

I hope that it helps.

Kind words, small deeds, sound advice.

Anything for you.


## ROAMING

Marvel at wonders.

Let curiosity roam.

Discover your world.


## SLEEPING DOGS

Let sleeping dogs lie.

You and the dog benefit.

You'll be happier.

## SEASONINGS

Not my cup of tea.

Add some sugar or honey.

Season to your taste.

## COGSWELL COGS

We all play our part.

One cog that turns the machine.

Keep the wheels turning.

## SMALL SAMPLES

Experience life.

Don't let it just flow past you.

Sample all flavors.

## CHECK YOUR VARIABLES

Path of "it depends".

It's filled with variables.

Not all's black and white.

## SPONGE

Children are sponges.

Take care in what they absorb.

Might need wringing out.


## EXCHANGES

Exchange ideas.

Try learning from each other.

Stubbornness aside.


## IN DUE TIME

Healing will take time.

It may feel slow or stagnant.

But it's a process.


## HOW TO PROCEED

Choose to do nothing.

That's exactly what you change.

Now how to proceed?

## **SWEPT AWAY**

Do what you enjoy.

Let passion sweep you away.

Lost in the moment.

## **DAM SON!**

You're swimming upstream.

The current is just too strong.

I'll build you a dam.

## **SHARED EXPERIENCES**

Important to you.

Then, important to me too.

We'll share joys and pains.

## **ECHOES**

Echoes are the past.

That which once was coming back.

Listen or close ears.

## **CARRIED**

Bucket filled with hate.

No room for anything else.

Dump or get new pail.


## **DISTURBANCE IN THE FORCE**

Your comfort disturbed.

It is going to happen.

How will you respond?


## **SHIFTED**

Give time to adjust.

A sudden change can be tough.

You are not alone.


## **GOOD ENOUGH**

There's no perfection.

We just do the best we can.

And that's good enough.

## WANTED

Want to feel wanted.

That's just us being human.

What's so wrong with that?

## THE PAYOFF

Your perseverance.

Eventually pays off.

At least in some ways.

## BARK AWAY

Go and lick your wounds.

Begin the healing process.

Bark another day.

## LINES DRAWN

Ethical lines crossed.

Push back on all encroachers.

Play some good defense.

## TO BE COOL

You want to be "cool".

Do what you enjoy doing.

Be your own person.

## WHAT THE SHELL

Outgrowing your shell.

You need more room for growing.

Inevitable.

## HALF THE BATTLE

Have things to work on.

Knowing you do is step one.

Proceed to step two.

## SINKING SHIPS

The ship is sinking.

Start expelling the water.

Be prepared to swim.

## REACHING

Friendly, helping hands.

Extend so far and then cramp.

Take some time to stretch.


## SOMETHING > NOTHING

Injustice prevails-

When good people do nothing.

Take up the mantle.


## THE VIEW

On uphill battle.

It's a struggle and you're tired.

Think of the top view.


## ABOUT LEARNING

Yeah, mistakes were made.

Learn from them and then move on.

This is how we grow.

## TEAM EFFORT

Burdens carried well.

Does not mean they're not heavy.

Lend a helping hand.


## NOW SHOWING

A complete shit show.

Stick it out and make changes.

Or, leave theater.


## SHAWL OF ENVY

The shawl of envy.

It's not a good look on you.

Try on something else.


## ON PURPOSE

A sense of purpose.

It's what we all want to feel.

Find and protect it.

## NOVELTY

Try repeatedly.

If you want it, go get it.

Don't fear novelty.

## WALK THIS WAY

Know to walk away.

Cannot change everybody.

Change your reaction.

## CENTERED

Sit and close your eyes.

Ignore all that's around you.

Focus on breathing.

## REVELATIONS

They'll reveal themselves.

Listen to what people say.

It will define them.

## HERE'S A LIGHT

A problem not seen.

That's a problem not dealt with.

Help by shedding light.

## FORECAST

Weather changes fast.

Don't get caught out in the storm.

Make sure you're prepared.

## TEACHABLE MOMENTS

It has been a blast.

Have we all learned something new?

Go and teach others.

## A NEW HOPE

Our time has ended.

Hope you've gleaned something while here.

It's why I wrote this.

*Special Thanks to my family, friends, and to all those who supported me through this.*

Sources Cited:

http://www.haikusyllablecounter.com/

https://www.howmanysyllables.com/

https:// http://www.syllablecount.com/

Made in the USA
Middletown, DE
14 January 2020